Song of the Shulammite

Roisin Rzeznik

Song of the Shulammite

Copyright © 2012 Roisin Rzeznik
Copyright © 2004 Roisin Rzeznik

All rights reserved.

ISBN-13:978-0615617466
ISBN-10:0615617468

Song of the Shulammite

Dedicated to:
My Savior; My Light, My Refuge, My Rock, My Strength, My Rainbow, My Friend, My Hero, My Lord, MY EVERYTHING!!!!!!!!!!!!!

-Roisin

CONTENTS

Acknowledgements i

Excerpt: Unseen Sorrow	1
Praising God	2
Passion and Pain	4
Break Free	5
Knowledge	6
Answer	7
Forget Me Not	8
Too Many Years	9
I Believe	10
45 Heartstrings	11
45 Beautiful Heartstrings	12
Everyday Too	13
We	14
Pray	15
Sweet Devotion	16
Shattered Rose	17
Amazing Grace	19
Battle Cry	20

Let it Ring	22
You're Everything	23
Fossil	24
Answered Prayers	25
Unconditional Love	26
To Be	28
Pure Love	29
Coming Home	30
Closer	31
From on High	32
Thank You	33
Waiting	34
Still Waters	35
Point of Grace	36
On His Mind	37
This Love	39
The Rhythm of Time	40

Song of the Shulammite

Reprinted for Joe Elliott; in loving memory of Joe Sr.

© Copyright The Bobby Sands Trust; The Rhythm of Time
© Copyright The Bobby Sands Trust; Unseen Sorrow

All Rights Reserved

Used by permission

ACKNOWLEDGMENTS

Thank you to all of my beautiful children for their love and heartfelt contributions to my world and Jesus a Mere Image...

My sweet grandbaby

Bobby Sands Trust

Joe

My Grandmothers, Grandfathers, and Uncle Paul for their love, patience, and kindness.

"Anam Chara, Domani è oggi...Amore Eterno"

My Extended family, whom love at all times...

You know who you are!

"Thank You"
Jesus

The Tolerant Twilight Singers

Roibeárd Gearóid Ó Seachnasaigh

Bobby Sands

"The Woman Cried"

Song of the Shulammite

AN EXCERPT FROM:

UNSEEN SORROW

BY
BOBBY SANDS

"Her tears fall in the darkness as the rain falls in the night,
Silvery tears like silvery rain, hidden out of sight.
The stars fall from her eyes like floating petals from the sky,
Is there no one in all this world who hears this woman cry?

A simple little flitting dreamy thought has stirred this woman's heart.
The golden sleepy dream of yesterdays before they were apart.
What comfort can there be found for a petal so fair and slim
Alone in a forest dark of sorrow she weeps again for him?"

-Bobby Sands

PRAISING GOD

The best way to start the day
Praising God
The best way to start the day
Praising God
The best way to start the day
Keeping it simple
The only way
The best way I know how
"Simply Pray"-"Simply Pray"
The only way
He will carry you through
Don't waste precious time
Always on my mind
He carries me through everyday
Don't waste your precious time
Always by my side carrying me through
Holding my hand as I make my way back to You
Over the mountains He allows me to climb
Always on my mind-He carries me through
Precious is our time
When all seems complete
At days end
I sing praise
To my very special Friend
Prayer, praise and thanks I do send

Saturated with love
My dear dear friend
Love Love Sweet Love
My love can never…
Never coming close to the love sent from above…
Nowhere near His ceaseless gifts
Sent from above
His ceaseless Love
Ceaseless Love
Ceaseless gifts of Love
I love You Lord
I try everyday
Never coming close
I cry everyday
No match for His ceaseless love
Oh, your mighty gift of love
Sent from above

PASSION AND PAIN

Love in the night
Arms around you
Wrapped in emotion
Like waves in the ocean
Lord does he ever call out for me

For Roisin

BREAK FREE

You can run
But you can not hide
As loneliness is filling you up inside
Pain and Pride
Chained to your side
Are a homely bride
Break Free-Break Free
On angels' wings
His love flows like molten gold
Let it fill your heart
Like a fountain through your veins
Let his love fill you inside
Wash away the pain
Throw away the pride
Throw away the burdens
They keep you hollow inside

KNOWLEDGE

No more longing
Free from wronging
Innocence is bliss
Love-Life-Live
Love beyond our knowledge
An everlasting eternal kiss
I love You
With you in my life
I've never been happier

ANSWER

In the darkness
In the darkness
We always feel a need to fight
So we can survive
Conquering
Conquering the giant
A primal need
He was there an answer to your prayer
He's been seeking you out
For your eyes to see
Behold-
The beauty
The tranquility
Is this just a fantasy
Is there far more to see
In your heart you have no doubt
In the darkness
Conquering
Conquering the giant
A primal need

FORGET ME NOT

Now and forever
A gift from above
Hope-Faith-Peace-Love
Love from a very special Dove
"Forget-Me-Not"
Cry Holy!
Cry Holy Holy Holy!
Holy Holy Holy!
Cry Holy Holy Holy!
I love You Lord!
I Love You Lord!

The best is yet to come...

TOO MANY YEARS

Two years
Two years too long
Friends kept apart…
Ready for a brand new start
Begin looking for that horizon
Something to focus your eyes on.
A gift of unknown splendor
The greatest One of all
A true and pure heart so tender
He was there to catch us
Taking the fall
Heed His call
Listen to the angels sing
He's here for us
As we soar on eagle's wings

I BELIEVE

I believe
The best is yet to come
I believe
You are the only One
I believe
You are the Truth-the Light-the Way
I believe
The words-every word-You say
I believe
I believe in the Holy Ghost
I believe
I believe in the One that loves me most
I believe
I believe in you
I believe in Love
I believe in You!
I believe!!!

45 HEARTSTRINGS

Heartstrings covered in morning dew
Here I am dreaming
Dreaming of You
Shield my eyes
Show me your glory
Paint my sky
My Lord so Holy
Let me see the twinkling in Your eyes
Heartstrings flowing with morning dew
Never let me stray
Forever I want to walk with you
Heartstrings singing-dancing in the morning dew
No gift greater than being loved
Loved by You!

45 BEAUTIFUL HEARTSTRINGS

Heartstrings covered in morning dew
As a star
Twinkles in Your eyes
Here I am dreaming
Dreaming of You
Shield my eyes
Show me Your glory
Paint my skies
My Lord so holy
Heartstrings flowing with morning dew
Let me see the twinkling in your eyes
Show me Your love so true
Never let me stray
Rediscovering You
Forever I want to walk
Walk with You
Heartstrings dancing in the morning dew
No gift greater than being loved
Loved by You

EVERYDAY TOO

Too many years
Years too long
Friends kept apart…
Ready for a brand new start
Begin looking for that horizon-
Something to focus your eyes on
A gift of unknown splendor
The greatest one of all
A true and pure heart so tender…
He was there to catch us
Taking the fall
Heed his call
Listen to the angels sing
He's here for us
As we soar on eagle's wings
A love beyond all
Standing tall
As we emerge from the cocoon that is Christ's
How beautiful our wings-
We know on sight it was pure love-
Each one for the other
Unselfishly bringing us back into His arms
The arms of our Creator and dear Friend Jesus-
Forever knowing
Without You Lord these wings of love would never be
showing
As the winds of change blow
He is leading us where we need to go

WE

As we emerge from the cocoon that is Christ's;
With our beautiful wings-
We know
On sight that it was pure love
Each one for the other-
Unselfishly bringing us back into the arms of our Creator
And dear Friend,
Jesus
-Forever knowing-
Without You Lord these wings of love would never be showing-
So on with Christ toward our destiny
As the winds of change blow
We thankfully go!

PRAY

I saw you today
It stirred my senses
Eased my soul
A love like this should bring down fences
And
Take back everything evil stole
Forget me not
For there are so many things
Things we need to share
And long to say
But
For now let it all fade away
As we finally clasp hands and pray:
Lord bless us indeed
Push our borders out
Allow them to recede
Let your glory shine
In and out of time
Strengthen our bond
With Your hand upon us
Allow our love to grow
More and more everyday
Keep us from evil
Never let us stray

SWEET DEVOTION

My Lord, My God
You are all I love
You saved
You healed
Helping him see
A bright destiny
You helped him learn
Held him tight
It was Your voice he heard
The voice of truth
Piercing the darkness
Ringing through the night
A reminder of youth
Now he's free to fly
Soaring on eagles' wings
He will never die

SHATTERED ROSE

Love never fails-Love Never Dies
Angel Girl-Angel Girl
Why do you cry
Love has no end
Angel Girl-Angel Girl
Dry your eyes
Love will always survive
He's on his way home-Home to stay
When you feel it- no part of you will want to hide
He'll never stray
Let him give you his hand
His heart has already led the way
You see
He's been here-He's been there
But He's never found another better
Watching you has become a treasure
Running into your arms his dream
He sees you as no other
He's there but you haven't seen him
He stays well behind the scene
You maybe catch a glimpse
Quickly dismissing it as your mind
You feel the nearness of his touch
Longing for his kiss
Soon you'll be entwined
Your new life-Eternal bliss

Angel Girl-Angel Girl
God is holding you tight
As you grasp those dreams
It's going to be alright
Angel Girl-Angel Girl
They are far closer than they seem
Watching waiting
For the light to shine
In your eyes
In perfect time
Angel Girl-Angel Girl
How deep the love
How beautifully it thrives
Angel Girl-Angel Girl
Wipe those tears from your eyes
Look up-Look to the skies
Angel Girl-Angel Girl
Dry your eyes
Love will always survive

AMAZING GRACE-LOST WITHOUT A TRACE

Confused-tortured-misguided- and used
Causing hurt keeps them amused.
Voices-Voices reeling in her head
Beaten broken left for dead
Tell me what does it take to be set free
What does it take
Tell me what does it take
Who holds the magic key
Have they no shame
Can anyone see- Can't anyone see
Consumption by eternal flame
Any other heart would condemn them-
How cruelly they maim
Amazing Grace- lost without a trace
Love is as strong as death
Oh, can't you see
They murdered him-They murdered me
Why can't anyone see; They murdered me
Make you a star, Yeah you'll go far
A captive in your own body
Mind control
Don't you know
Their evil suppressing my soul
Why doesn't anyone see-Can't anyone see
Watch
True Love
True Love breaks free
Ready to fulfill her destiny

BATTLE CRY

Tears in your eyes
No where left to turn
The loneliness- the pain
What does it all mean
Is there anyone who can understand-
The soul's silent scream
He knows the soul's battle cry
It's ringing in His ears
Call on Him-Call on His name
He's been waiting there-waiting for years
He commands even the stars dancing in the night sky
He will never forsake us
He loves at all times
When I feel my soul screaming
"Don't leave me wondering why"
I call on Him with the age old battle cry
Wiping the tears from my eyes like no other
Be still and know
He is a God of wonder
He's leading me beside still water
He makes me feel like I'm His one and only daughter
Call on His name
He will love you like no other
In Him you will find your peace
Providing protection from all evil
God loves like no other
Favoring the least

Battle cry
The cry of the ages
Louder than the eagle that screams on high
Battle cry
Calling out to the Great Protector
From Him no man can hide his evil ways
No pity for the man who chooses to betray
For our Lord has equipped us
With this brilliant Battle Cry
Reigning from the heavens
He will never let us die
Battle Cry
Battle Cry
I call Him with the age old Battle Cry

LET IT RING

Love
Unconditional love
Show it-
Know it-
Let it ring out in the night
No way-
You're not giving up this fight
The world knows it
Show it-
They know it-
Aren't going to lose
Won't lose this fight…

YOU'RE EVERYTHING

You're everything to me
More than my eyes can see
You're everything to me
Far greater than any fantasy
You're my beautiful reality
You're everything to me
And...
I Love you

FOSSIL

Love-
Come on back to me
Lost & alone
A discard of summer
Like a leaf
Faded-Worn-Forgotten
Falling-Falling
Into icy waters
Frozen
Suspended
In the Waters of Time
Destiny-
Like an unanswered question
Thy Will
Be my guide

ANSWERED PRAYERS

I thank my Lord
For the rainbows and butterflies
The flowers and trees
For all the wisdom and knowledge I find
When I'm on my knees
I thank Him for you
As I walk…
Through those trees
Hearing the wind whisper
Oh, how glorious
Oh, how my Lord cares
His love comes shinning through
Warming my soul
I know He holds you
I thank Him
As we climb these stairs
Thank You Jesus for answered prayers

UNCONDITIONAL LOVE- A VALENTINE

Deep in your heart there is a place
A place for me;
A place with you
Though the miles separate
To lose you now would be a disgrace
It's time to let the world see
The love we share
Always in your heart
There is no better fate
No one else knows the secret hidden there
Let's move beyond all that tears us apart
Come home before it's too late
Losing you now is more than I can bear
The moments together so few
Though I can feel you there
I long to touch your face
Hold your hand
Hear your voice
Build our castles without the sand
Loving you has always been my choice
Deep in my heart there is a place
A place for you;
A place with me

We both know that this is true
On the Lord we shall wait
That is what we must do
Worth the wait
Across time and space
Soon we'll be together
In our place
Me and You
Sharing our love so true

TO BE

To be held in the arms of love
To be cared for
Swaddled in love and light
All this sent from above
You care for me
Such an undeserving dove
So hard to accept
Thank You Lord for not giving up
It's easy to lose sight
Hard to trust hope
By faith alone…
Through all the storms
You are my shining Star
You hold me with all your might
Priceless and precious
Your Love
No matter how near or far
Through Your power, love and light
I know I won't lose this fight

PURE LOVE

The colors of the rainbow
So radiant-rich and exact
Designed by gifted hands with love
As it is written, "Be still and know…"
A brilliant reminder of a heavenly pact
A message sent from above
A message steeped in love
Pure Love

COMING HOME

Touching fingertip to fingertip
I feel the thundering of your heart
Pulsing in my hands
How glorious your touch
I need You
I love You so much
Lovingly caressing my face
Opening my eyes
Wiping away the tears of pain
Your hands of grace
Walking with You destiny bound
On a road where our dreams will be fulfilled
Headed to a place where only tears of joy remain
Asking how long must the patience last
How long the wait
To be in your presence
The One whose love has saved me
That is where I want to be
Oh to fall into Your arms like a child
It's Your face I long to see
Your love grasping my soul
Instantly-
I know everything will be alright
You whisper, "Be still and know…"

CLOSER

Friendship
Through it you'll see
How wonderful life can truly be
Enter in
Arms wide-open
Love-Joy
More than you were ever hoping
If you could see
What's so very apparent to me
It has been since before
Now and Forever
Come on- Open the door
Welcome to Forevermore
Where the joy is contagious
Real-True-Faithful Love
Unconditional completeness
Mercy and grace from above
I must confess- I've never been so blessed
Lord you are…
My Morning Star
Nothing about this love is too outrageous
Without Your Love Lord…
My life would be page-less

FROM ON HIGH

Ringing from on high
It's true
Shining from above
It's You
Coursing through my soul
I feel so new
Pounding in my heart
Sweetness in the morning dew
It's beautiful being loved by You

THANK YOU; THANK YOU

Lord God- I love You so
Thank You for all the gifts You bestow-
Thank You Lord for those times when You chose to say No!
Thank You for showing me when I had further to go…
Lord, I love You so!!!
You're everything to me-
More than my eyes can see-
"Lord of all creation"
Lord of my heart and soul
Thank You for cheering me on when I have
Further to go…

WAITING

What was I waiting for
This broken Rose needs you
NOW…like never before
Lord, Jesus I hear You knocking
Please help me open this door
Let me sidle up next to You
What are we waiting for
Rushing into your open arms
In Your glory
I'm finally home
Safely away from all that harms
Oh, the way You've healed my heart
I could never ask for more
Let my Lord help you turn the key
He will open the door
Broken and lame
What are you waiting for
Let Him open that door
He loves you more
What are you waiting for

STILL WATERS

Tears welling in my eyes and running down my cheek-
Seeing the grandeur of what the Lord has created
There are no earthly words to speak-
I think of you-
Wondering where it is you lay your head to sleep-
Gazing at the ocean-
I wonder if you realize-
My love for you runs this deep

POINT OF GRACE

It's not a state of mind as everyone cares to suggest
It is in fact a point of grace
I cannot wait to see You face to face

ON HIS MIND
(Living Soul)

Something in the way he looks at me
Makes me want to hold him tight
Something in the way he looks at me
Lets me know everything will be alright
Be alright
He looks at me
Calming my internal fears
Something in the way he looks at me
Lets me know he will forever be near
Forever be dear
Hold on to me-Hold on to me
Don't give up
Now we're back to where we started
Don't give up
Something in the way he looks at me
Causes my spirit to heal
I can feel him here
Something in the way he looks at me
Let's me know it's all so real
Wonderfully real
Don't give up on what you feel
Something in the way he looks at me
Lets me know my soul is guarded
Something in the way he looks at me
Lets me know we'll never be parted
He will never leave me broken hearted

Something in the way he looks at me
Eases the internal fight
Without him something just isn't right
I know within my soul God Himself has lifted him
Far beyond my sight
Though I can't see him
I can feel him in the air tonight
Close my eyes and feel him tonight
Not by my power, but by His might
Everything is going to turn out- Right

THIS LOVE

This is a love that is going to last
This kind of love happens so fast
It's a sweet romance
Entwined in an endless dance
This is a love without end
I need no promise to know
Wherever I am you go
A carpenter's hands
The detailed plans
The love just grows and grows
With you there is no fear
No foes
I've discovered Heaven on Earth
In the form of a Man
Let Him touch your heart
You will understand
This is a love that is going to last
This kind of love happened so fast
It's a sweet romance
Enjoy the endless dance

The Rhythm of Time
By
Bobby Sands

There's an inner thing in every man,
Do you know this thing my friend?
It has withstood the blows of a million years,
And will do so to the end.

It was born when time did not exist,
And it grew up out of life,
It cut down evil's strangling vines,
Like a slashing searing knife.

It lit fires when fires were not,
And burnt the mind of man,
Tempering leadened hearts to steel,
From the time that time began.

It wept by the waters of Babylon,
And when all men were a loss,
It screeched in writhing agony,
And it hung bleeding from the Cross.

It died in Rome by lion and sword,
And in defiant cruel array,
When the deathly word was 'Spartacus,'
Along the Appian Way.

It marched with Wat the Tyler's poor,
And frightened lord and king,
And it was emblazoned in their deathly stare,
As e'er a living thing.

Song of the Shulammite

It smiled in holy innocence,
Before conquistadors of old,
So meek and tame and unaware,
Of the deathly power of gold.

It burst forth through pitiful Paris streets,
And stormed the old Bastille,
And marched upon the serpent's head,
And crushed it 'neath its heel.

It died in blood on buffalo plains,
And starved by moons of rain,
Its heart was buried in Wounded Knee,
But it will come to rise again.

It screamed aloud by Kerry lakes,
As it was knelt upon the ground,
And it died in great defiance,
As they coldly shot it down.

It is found in every light of hope,
It knows no bounds nor space,
It has risen in red and black and white,
It is there in every race.

It lies in the hearts of heroes dead,
It screams in tyrants' eyes,
It has reached the peak of mountains high,
It comes searing 'cross the skies.

It lights the dark of this prison cell,
It thunders forth its might,
It is 'the undauntable thought,' my friend,
That thought that says 'I'm right!'

ABOUT THE AUTHOR

Roisin Rzeznik

Roisin Rzeznik is best known by her pseudonym Roisin (Van gogh-Rzeznik). She is a Midwest, Milwaukee, Chicago area artist, writer, photographer, pragmatic philosopher, activist, and humanitarian. She has four children whom are now grown and a grandson.

 She enjoys creating....

Roisin is a versatile artist working with many mediums and experimental techniques...most prevalent are her paintings and an occasional block print or rare drawing. Her focus is on contemporary art, abstract expressionism, research, visual rhyme, and poetry.

A tremendous lover of the archaic, prose, and art world-wide. The artist was inspired at an early age by her mentors and their willingness to indulge, experiment, and instruct in a broad, diverse, and eclectic range of art, technique, and philosophy.

Over the years Roisin has spent her time highlighting Fair Trade, fighting for human rights, women's rights, children's rights, racial congruity, the abolition of extreme poverty, Aids, Malaria, human trafficking, and Genocide.

Roisin is known for often crediting her greatest loves as influences including God Himself; music as her muse and those whom create it.

Roisin credits Greg Dulli as the magical masterful genius whom constantly drives her to explore her artistic direction and often fill page upon page with verse. Of which, Filthy Sleaze (Out Damn Spot), her latest poem, which is said to illuminate the darkness surrounding human trafficking and other global and societal ills has been compared to Allen Ginsberg's Howl.

Roisin harbors a deep belief that, "Global Peace and Unity are achievable; They are a tangible gift from the Almighty."

www.ingramcontent.com/pod-product-compliance
Lightning Source LLC
Chambersburg PA
CBHW071801040426
42446CB00012B/2663